Old Organization, New Tricks:

Five Practical Keys to Unlocking a Learning Organization

Shannon Graves
Richard Hoefer, Ph.D.

The Center for Advocacy, Nonprofit and Donor Organizations (CAN-DO)
University of Texas at Arlington School of Social Work
211 S. Cooper Street • PO Box 19129 Arlington, TX 76019

Find us online at www.uta.edu/can-do

This document is authored by and is the copyrighted material of Shannon Graves and Richard Hoefer.

© 2013 Shannon Graves and Richard Hoefer

Usage Guidelines
You do not have permission to copy, redistribute, or republish this work without the express written consent of the authors.

Find us online at www.uta.edu/can-do to access a constantly growing library of resources for nonprofit advocacy and human services management.

Foreword

The Journey You're Embarking On: What You're About to Learn

Congratulations on your purchase of this guidebook to your organization's future. Welcome to a future where your colleagues, your board, and your organization itself approach each day as an opportunity to get better, to improve, and to learn! This book, while short and easy to understand, will be your step-by-step companion on an exciting journey to becoming a learning organization.

In these pages, you will find information on five locks that prevent progress in many organizations. These locks keep you, your staff and your organization from maximizing your potential. Perhaps you recognize some of these in your agency and **hate** the way they are holding you back:

- Nothing EVER changes
- Everything is always about the short-term
- The new people we hire are smart, but don't "get" us very well
- It's IMPOSSIBLE to get support for new ways of doing things
- Everyone is busy doing their OWN thing—and we never know what that is!

If you experience any of these nagging and demoralizing issues on the job, this book, *Old Organizations, New Tricks* will help you unlock potential you didn't know was there. The Five Keys you'll read about will lead you to

- Examine the present, imagine the future, and move forward

- See both the forest and the trees so you can thrive
- Make choices now to reap large benefits later
- Hire people who will fit in, contribute and stay around because they love working in your organization
- Ensure growth opportunities to build a better team
- Uncover and update operating practices that have outlived their usefulness
- Use generative dialogue to uncover faulty decisions, before you lose time, money, staff, and community support
- Guide, mold and cultivate a shared vision of excellence
- Implement the lessons you and your staff members have learned from experiences in your organization

And much more.

Again, congratulations for investing a small amount of money now, to reap significant benefits later. Let's get going!

Shannon
Rick

Table of Contents

Introduction: About this Report 4
Key 1: Expand Your Horizons 8
Key 2: Invest in People 13
Key 3: Retire Outdated Paradigms 17
Key 4: Cultivate a Shared Vision 21
Key 5: Tap In to the Collective 24
Wrap-up and Summary 28
Can We Do Something More for You? 29
Learn More with Video Resources by CAN-DO 30
Excerpt from "Your Organization's Riveting Story" 31

Introduction: About this Report

Is Your Organization a Learning Organization?

Diane works at EveryPlace, a nonprofit organization just like many you might know. EveryPlace serves people in the community who are in need. Most of the staff and volunteers care about helping people and come to EveryPlace wanting to make a difference and do important work. Diane has worked at EveryPlace now for seven years and has seen many changes: several staff have left the organization for new jobs and new staff have taken their places, the number of clients served has increased each year, and donations have helped to make improvements to the office space like a fresh coat of paint and new parking.

On the other hand, lots of things have *not* changed. With a few exceptions, the same programs have been in existence since the organization's inception, and many are operating in the exact same way that they were when Diane started seven years ago. As a senior employee, Diane helps train many of the new staff members that seem in constant influx at EveryPlace. She trains them to do things the same way they have been done before – the same way she was trained to do them. At staff meetings, the managers report out on program successes, and on birthdays, everyone gathers for cake.

EveryPlace is a nice place to work, and Diane knows she is making a difference for the clients. However, she can't help but wonder if she is really making the difference that she *could* be, and no longer feels challenged or inspired by her work. As she begins to observe more closely, it seems as though there is an invisible force holding EveryPlace back from real change or growth. New ideas are frequently countered with an emphasis on "how things are done around here." Deep down, Diane wants to grow and she wants her work to be meaningful. But she can't help feeling that the doors at EveryPlace are locked tight against change.

Maybe you know of an organization like EveryPlace. Maybe *your* organization is very similar. Intentions are good, and solid work is being done. But innovation, change, and the opportunity for individuals to make high quality personal contributions to the organization are rare. As a result, many things are being done the same way they were five years ago… or ten… or twenty. Without being able to make a meaningful contribution, staff come and go. In fact, when other options don't pan out, sometimes staff come and go and come again. When they do, they are able to pick up right where they left off. Do you see a problem with this picture?

Perhaps you know of a different kind of organization – one which is innovative and adaptable. It takes risks, and sometimes makes mistakes. But it sees each challenge as an opportunity to learn something important. As a result, it keeps getting *better and better.* This is a special type of organization, "where people continually expand their capacity to create the results they truly desire, where new and expansive patterns of thinking are nurtured, where collective aspiration is set free, and where people are continually learning to see the whole together." These are the words of Peter Senge (1990, p. 3) who first coined the term *learning organization* and inspired tens of thousands of questions and answers about what it means for organizations to learn and exactly how we can help them to do so.

This short report is also inspired by Senge's ideas, and it draws on the work of many others who have written about and studied this curious phenomenon before and after him. This report simplifies some basic characteristics of learning organizations and suggests practical exercises that you can implement right away in order to start leading your organization down a new path – a path that is not without potholes or forks in the road but which nonetheless moves *onward and upward* to higher ground.

How to Get the Most from This Report

We believe that the contents of this report can be deeply meaningful for your organization. While the length is short and the language is simple, each section represents a bigger body of work that remains for you to explore and learn from. View the Five Keys presented in the following pages as a powerful starting place for an ongoing journey with your organization. When you have read all five, it is likely that one will stand out as an area in which your organization is currently facing an opportunity for growth. Start there. Implement the strategies provided and be courageous in creating your own exercises for bringing the principle to life. Remember: Even if one technique falls flat, it is no longer to be viewed as a failure, but as an opportunity for *learning*.

As you work through the Five Keys, we highly recommend starting a Lessons Log. The Lessons Log is a journal in which you record your lessons learned – lessons that now guide both your personal leadership and the work of your organization. See the inset box for a suggested format for each entry of your Lessons Log. Once you've written, return often and review your lessons learned. Especially when you plan to embark on a path you've been down before, your journal entries can serve as an invaluable reference.

Try This! Keep a Lessons Log

Today / this week / this month / this year, I / we learned!

- I / we tried ___.
- What *worked* about it was ___.
- What *didn't work* about it was ___, because ___.
- In the future, I / we will improve by ___. (Be specific!)

Note: If your effort was a team effort, ask your team to help you answer the questions above. Don't worry, we'll talk more about team debriefings later in Key 5!

However you use this report, we hope that it will inspire you to think about your organization's work in a new way. We also hope that if you have any questions about the content here or if find yourself facing challenges that are bigger than the scope of this report, that you will reach out to CAN-DO to have your questions addressed and learn how training and technical assistance from CAN-DO (www.uta.edu/can-do) may be able to help YOU. Now, let's explore the Five Keys of leading an organization that never stops learning.

Learning Organizations

Key 1: Expand Your Horizons

One critical lock that many organizations face is a limited frame of view. These organizations fail to see important opportunities or threats confronting them in the larger environment. They may have few partnerships in the community and an over emphasis on the internal workings of the agency. They rarely adapt new ideas from outside and rarely influence other organizations.

Organizations with a limited frame of view are also likely to make short-sighted decisions. They may make choices that seem good now but that are not beneficial to the organization in the long run.

An important characteristic that learning organizations have in common is that staff are tuned in to the larger context in which the organization exists. Your organization does not operate in a bubble, but is one organism within an interdependent ecosystem. Recognizing the interconnectedness of people, organization, and environment cultivates a broader viewpoint for both taking in innovation and influencing others. This "big picture" thinking allows you to both see the whole forest that contains your tree and to think long-term about the growth of your organization.

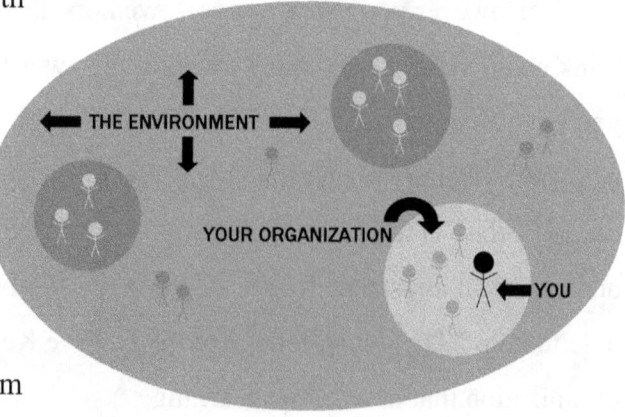

Step 1.1: See the Whole

Leaders of learning organizations recognize that their organization is just one moving part of a larger, complex, working machinery which includes government and regulatory agencies, the cultural and social norms of the community, interest groups, researchers and universities, external funding sources, pools of potential volunteers and staff, and client groups. Organizations which have trouble seeing past their own doors struggle to respond effectively to the changing community environment and make unnecessary mistakes by failing to learn from the opportunities around them. Ask the following questions of yourself and your staff:

- What does science and research say about the effectiveness of our policies, programs, and practices?
- Which organizations are prospering in our unique community environment? What sets them apart?
- What evidence is there that our community supports our vision and our plan to achieve it?
- Is there any evidence that our community does ***not*** fully support our efforts or that our clients are needs are ***not*** fully met?
- How effectively are we using funding sources, training and development opportunities, collaborative opportunities, or other external resources available in our environment?
- What other entities in our community also interact frequently with our clients? Is there anything new they can tell us about our clients' needs or the effectiveness of our services?

- Have we recognized and responded to opportunities to influence our environment on a larger scale (beyond individual clients)?

Step 1.2: Think Long Term

Just as it is important to see beyond the geographic boundaries of the organization, it is also essential to look past the present moment and into the future. Learning organizations are often perceived as highly innovative and forward-thinking. This is because they understand that key investments *now* can yield exponential results in the future. Because it is challenging to see the long-range outcomes of decision making, organizations frequently neglect long term investments in favor of short term, tangible gains. Consider an organization that makes cuts in their development budget to improve the current bottom line. What is the likely result of this decision next year, or for the next few years?

While no one can predict what the future, thinking about what is most likely to occur as a result of current decisions is an important part of a long-term, investment-focused mentality. Be sure to ask "What actions taken now are likely to yield significantly larger results later, for good or ill?" A small shift in course now leads to a big change in direction later.

In addition, learning organizations are highly tuned in to how the community is likely to change in the next five, ten, twenty, and fifty years. As a result, they can create a meaningful plan for strategic growth of the organization itself. Here are some questions you can ask yourself and your staff to prompt a long range strategic planning process:

Learning Organizations

- How is our community likely to change in the next five years? Ten years? Twenty years?
- Who will live in our community? What will their needs be?
- What needs exist now that may be eliminated or less important in the future?
- How are funding sources and other external resources likely to change?
- How are priorities in government and regulatory agencies likely to shift?

Most importantly, ask yourselves whether you will be prepared for these realities. What can you do *now* to plan for the future? Here's an example. Suppose you anticipate that shifts in government priorities are likely to reduce the availability of tax dollars, grants, and government contracts for your area of service. If your budget currently relies on a large percentage of government funding, then a forward-thinking strategy would be to diversify funding sources for your agency as soon as possible and moderate this risk. Or, you may decide to invest resources in advocating for the importance of your services to the community and relevant elected officials.

Identify ways to not only lessen risk associated with upcoming changes, but also to take advantage of arising opportunities for innovation. What if your agency was first to predict an evolving need for a new service in your community, and in fact was already prepared with the infrastructure and expertise to address this need by the time others became aware of it? In essence, learning organizations are visionaries. Developing a long-term vision will invariably lead you to Key 2 – hiring people with vision themselves and investing in them generously as critical organizational resources.

> ### *Have You Already Answered These Questions?*
>
> Many organizations go through planning processes to answer these types of questions. One common approach is called SWOT Analysis, which stands for Strengths, Weaknesses, Opportunities and Threats analysis.
>
> If you've already conducted a SWOT analysis, "Congratulations!" and good work. This lays the foundation for becoming a learning organization. If you haven't yet done a SWOT Analysis, you'll find it extremely useful as you become a learning organization. Too busy to do this all on your own? The experts at CAN-DO can help your organization with this type of consulting, saving you time in the process. Contact Dr. Rick Hoefer, CAN-DO Director, at rhoefer@uta.edu.

Key 2: Invest in People

Organizations are made up of people. Many organizations face a lock when they fail to place importance on selecting, developing, and honoring their team members in meaningful ways. These organizations are often marked by a lack of commitment and motivation among staff. Their working environments may be characterized by frequent conflict, apathy, or merely a casual, nonproductive attitude toward the work of the organization. The most highly effective and valued employees are drawn away to other organizations, where they can reach their full potential. As a result, these organizations have high rates of turnover. Time spent on hiring, training, and managing personnel issues takes away from the real work of the organization.

In effect, an organization's capacity to learn, grow, and innovate is only as strong as the capacity of its personnel to do so. Individuals working in an organization must be committed to personal and organizational growth in order to contribute to a culture of learning. While it may seem that you have limited control over the enthusiasm of your employees, in reality, you have a lot! By making strategic hiring decisions, contributing to employee development, and respecting relationships as a key organizational resource, you can create a team worthy of a learning organization.

Step 2.1: Hire for Substance over Skill

When we think about the desirable qualities of a new staff member, we may consider factors like these: experienced, knowledgeable, skilled in the delivery of services we provide. While these are worthy qualities, could it be that other attributes are more important? Emerging theories on personnel management suggest that hiring staff based on character and personal qualities is a better investment than hiring staff based exclusively on already obtained knowledge and skill. After all, content and practice skills can be taught and learned. It is much more challenging to teach employees to develop a learning-centered mindset, to demonstrate risk-taking, or to work effectively with a team.

In addition, employees who feel personally invested in the organization's vision are more likely to make high quality contributions. Consider which character traits best align with the mission and vision of your organization, as well as your commitment to becoming an innovative learning organization. Examples might include social- and self- awareness, creativity, strategic thinking, beneficence, or an interest in discovery. When filling positions within you organizations, ask candidates to respond to scenarios in which these traits might be used. Consider non-traditional candidates who are likely to be committed to your organization and its growth at a deeper level than simple match of service and experience.

Step 2.2: Develop Employees

Assuming that employees have high potential when hired, there is still an important demand for ongoing support and development of personnel. Employees who are interested in their own development – both within and outside the context of the organization – are more likely to be vital participants in the cultivation of a learning organization. Help employees create personal and professional development plans in which they set goals for increase of specific knowledge, skills, experiences, and other capacities which enable them to contribute to the organization's vision at a higher level. By demonstrating the organization's willingness to invest in its staff, you will also inspire a deeper commitment to working for the good of the organization.

A natural consequence of a desire to develop employees is that you and your board must devote resources to this step, *even when budgets are tight.* A focus on developing your employees will keep turnover low, motivation high, and the organization moving towards greater learning.

Step 2.3: Respect Relationships

Successfully developing and cultivating staff members requires a healthy respect for the importance of human relationships. Teams who feel a caring connection with one another and value each other's contributions are more easily able to take risks, work through conflicts, and make collective decisions. Leaders who prioritize and cultivate relationships are more readily able to foster the climate of trust and openness which is required for learning from mistakes. Take a genuine interest in people that you interact with on a daily basis – staff, volunteers, funders, community partners – and make a special effort to maintain an open, honest, and caring relationship with each.

> ***Try This!***
>
> ***Invest in Relationships by Exercising Gratitude***
>
> *One important way to practice valuing relationships with those around you is to take time to express your appreciation and gratitude for their contributions to your life and work. Who has helped your organization run smoothly, grow unexpectedly, or celebrate vividly this week? Send them a handwritten note that is specific and sincere. Let them know you value their contribution. Make this a weekly practice, and see what happens as a result.*

Key 3: Retire Outdated Paradigms

One of the strongest locks that inhibits many organizations from achieving excellence is also the hardest to see. An organization can easily become stagnant without even realizing that counteractive underlying beliefs are stopping up progress! Such organizations rely on a single way of thinking about things or doing things for far too long. In these organizations, inquiries about policies or practices are frequently answered with something like "That's the way we've always done it." Suggestions for even minor improvements are met with resistance. When change efforts are undertaken, the end result is that the same types of decisions are made – over and over again.

Many terms have been invented to describe the underlying assumptions and beliefs that drive our actions: paradigms, limiting beliefs, artifacts, mental models, schemas. Often, we remain unaware of these hidden thought patterns, but they continue to drive our ways of thinking, responding, and making decisions. Importantly, staff members in learning organizations are willing and able to recognize the paradigms driving thought, dialogue, and action, and discard them when they are not functional. By first uncovering your own limiting beliefs, you can help to clear the path for generative dialogue.

Step 3.1: Uncover Your Own Limiting Beliefs

Uncovering the assumptions behind your impulses can be a challenging exercise. These assumptions are often grounded in deeply rooted values and beliefs. Begin to identify and bring to light your own limiting beliefs through a questioning process. When a challenge or impasse is reached, ask "Why is it that I feel this way? What are the assumptions that are driving my ideas? Are these assumptions useful *here*, and are there other more accurate assumptions that might better serve me in this situation?"

Another helpful way to think about assumptions is using the "anchor and frame" metaphor. When making a decision, we each rely on both anchors and frames. Anchors are those grounding rules that keep us in a certain pattern of thinking. For instance, suppose that you see something in a store that you like, such as a suit, but you don't buy it because it costs "too much." You have anchor in your mind which sets the reasonable cost of a suit. In addition, you also employ frames – the contexts in which you are making the decision – to reinforce or change your anchor point. While you normally would consider a cost "too much" for a new suit, you may make a different decision when taking into account that your luggage was lost and you have an important meeting in the morning. The frames of "convenience" and "importance" now help to shape what is "too much." By identifying the anchors and frames you are using to make decisions, you can become more self-aware and accommodate new anchors and frames which help lead to better, more appropriate choices.

Step 3.2: Clear the Path for Generative Dialogue

Next, turn the microscope from yourself and onto your organization. During group discussions and decision-making opportunities, be on the lookout for anchors and frames that are driving dialogue of the group and individuals. Guide the group by pausing to inquire about and reflect upon the key assumptions that aren't being spoken.

One helpful exercise is to use "If, then" statements to clarify the paths of thought that are present. For instance, suppose that a team discussion results in recommendations to engage in more advertising of the organization's services. Possible assumptions underlying this suggestion include:

- IF we put an advertisement in the local paper, THEN many of our potential donors/clients will likely see it.
- IF people in the community see our ad, THEN they will choose to support or patronize our organization more frequently.
- IF we pay $300 for an ad, THEN we will receive more than $300 worth of benefit to the agency in the long-term.

Consider whether there are any false assumptions in these points. How many potential donors/clients are likely to see an ad in the proposed venue? What percentage is likely to respond with the desired behavior? Will the investment made by the organization result in an adequate benefit? Within the answers to these questions lie assumptions about the effectiveness of advertising, the popularity of the selected venue, and other beliefs and values.

Learning Organizations

After identifying underlying assumptions, look for opportunities to test assumptions. In this case, find out the readership of the local paper. Ask another organization who has recently advertised what benefit they have seen from the decision to do so. Look into the most recent management research to find out which advertising venues and messages are most effective in order to reach the goals you have in mind. As a team, decide which assumptions you can all agree on before making a decision. Clearing out the ones that the team does not agree on makes room for a dialogue that moves forward rather than around in circles. Now, innovative solutions can be proposed, and true creation can take place!

Try This!
Train Staff to Become "Myth Busters"

In the popular television show "Myth Busters," scientists take on popular myths and urban legends and test them in a laboratory to see whether they could be true. As you engage in generative dialogue with staff and uncover a faulty assumption, proudly display it on a list of "busted" myths. Challenge staff to add to the list and award prizes or public acclaim for major discoveries. Cultivate an attitude of critical inquiry and teach staff to question and problem solve in new ways.

Learning Organizations

Key 4: Cultivate a Shared Vision

Even organizations with a clear mission statement and vision statement can lack a shared vision – and without a shared vision, your organization's full potential remains locked up tight! In an organization where team members don't embrace a collective goal, personal objectives take precedence. In these organizations, staff may have a "What's in it for me?" mentality. Work teams may engage in turf wars or cliquish behavior: "Our program is better than your program!" And even individuals serving on the same work teams may have different ideas about what should be done and how. While the disruptiveness of this mentality may range from severe to minor, lack of a shared vision prevents the organization from the meaningful *growth* that can occur when everyone is in the same boat, on the same river, and rowing their paddles in the same direction.

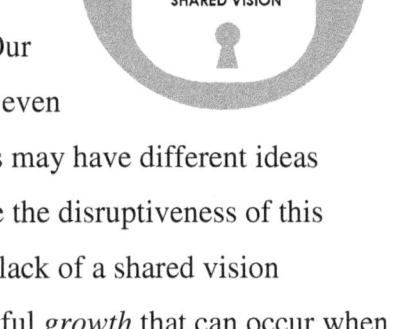

In order to become a leading, learning organization, your entire staff must not only support but *share* a vision about what the organization is achieving and where it is going in the future. A team experiencing this type of synergy finds and pursues new opportunities and ideas almost spontaneously. Rather than blocking or ignoring each other's efforts, the team is *for* each other and *for* a common vision of what the organization can do. In this key, the leader's task is to help cultivate this shared vision and to drive the pursuit of it.

Step 4.1: Cultivate, Don't Create

The shared vision of your organization is not necessarily the same as your vision statement, and as the leader, you cannot dictate the shared vision to others. Instead, people are committed to a shared vision because it reflects their personal vision. This is why it is important to hire staff who have a personal vision with some similarities to the organizational vision, and to invest in their growth through further development of their personal and professional selves (Key 2). But it goes beyond that!

As the leader, you have an important role in helping to guide and mold the vision. You can support a shared vision by expressing your own personal vision often, and more importantly, inviting others to do the same. What is their picture of the future that inspires them to contribute at a high level? What role do they see the organization playing in creating this future? When your team begins to speak up about their personal visions and explore connections between them, a shared vision can begin to form through the enthusiasm and mutual reinforcement of all members.

Step 4.2: Pursue the Vision

The organization's shared vision fuels learning by providing the motivation and energy for meaningful growth. Once your team has a collective picture of what it wants to create, help generate movement toward that goal by reinforcing the team's vision as often as possible. Clearly link daily tasks, organizational changes, and emerging opportunities to the collective vision. Make it obvious how decisions made at the upper levels of the organization are in alignment with the collective vision, and be genuinely open to feedback from staff when they appear unable to see the connection. Take the extra effort to ensure that team members are able to see the daily operations of the organization as a meaningful expression of the vision and to invest in them accordingly.

Set aside time in meetings where important decisions will be made to reconnect with the shared vision. One way to do this is by allowing staff to describe the vision in their own words and discuss how they see the current decision fitting in. Remember that this process isn't as simple as announcing the organization's official mission or vision statement. The shared vision is generated by the team and has a life of its own. Allow the team to reshape and recommit to it often through open dialogue.

Try This!
Create an Organizational Vision Board

Take time during a staff meeting to talk about the importance of visioning. Invite staff members to create a personal vision by creating a collage of words and images that speak to them. A traditional approach is to provide magazines, brochures, and other image-centric materials, along with scissors and glue. Staff members could even be asked to bring images along from outside. Afterward, designate a large posterboard or corkboard in an office common area as the organizational vision board. Encourage staff to add to it often as they see images that align with their vision of the organization and its goals. The board can serve as a visual reminder of your shared vision during challenging meetings and decision-making periods. (A web-based alternative could allow staff to pin images to a Pinterest wall, later projected onto a screen during meetings.)

Key 5: Tap In to the Collective

The final lock addressed by this report is a big one, and one that is best able to be tackled by organizations that have begun work on many or all of the keys discussed in the previous pages. This is because organizations with a big picture view, great staff, innovative ideas, and a shared vision may still fail to reach their full potential if they don't learn to actually act together as a team. An organization that is not accessing its collective power may have an excellent staff, but often doesn't use team members to their full potential. Team members hold back ideas that seem risky or unlikely to be supported by the group. This type of organization values how smoothly it functions and how well staff get along, but balks at signs of conflict or risk-taking.

By learning how to think, act, and create together without fear of failure or disagreement, your team can create significantly more than any one individual within it. A team which recognizes that he sum is greater than its parts has permission to encourage differences as an opportunity for growth and is willing to discuss and learn from their mistakes.

Step 5.1: Recognize the Sum is Greater than its Parts

In a famous exercise on collective wisdom, individuals are asked to guess the weight of an object or the number of tokens in a jar. While individual answers range from quite close to quite far off, the average of all responses reveals itself to be the closest guess. If you have ever experienced a team meeting in which ideas begin to flow freely, naturally correcting, supporting, and building onto one another in order to create a solution that is much better than any individual answer, then you have been witness to this same current of collective wisdom. A knowledgeable and well-trained team can easily outperform the individual.

Try This! Start a Virtual Think Tank

Wikipedia and Yahoo! Answers are essentially global online think tanks. Establish your own online forum where team members can post problems and solutions related to current projects.

Step 5-2: Encourage Differences... and Dissent

One of the reasons that teams are able to outperform individuals is that each group contains people with different backgrounds, experiences, and strengths. While the input of key individuals may shine at points in the process where their skills and knowledge are most relevant, the entire range of the group is required to solve the problem. High functioning teams value input from team members with diverse perspectives and areas of expertise.

Celebrating differences naturally means that disagreements will be present as well. Rather than avoiding signs of dissent, successful teams readily accept disagreement and conflict as healthy mechanisms of group cohesion. Imagine a scenario in which a few vocal team members often have similar viewpoints about the best path to take. Other members of the group have different, possibly innovative, ideas but they rarely contribute due to fear of dissenting from the group and triggering conflict, or feeling that their different ideas may not be valued.

In order to tap into the collective wisdom of the group, the leader must create a learning environment which is open, honest, and respectful.

- Ensure that all group members are prepared and have the opportunity to participate.
- Challenge group members on their lack of meaningful participation or their over-participation.
- Model giving honest feedback, disagreeing respectfully, and embracing conflict as a learning opportunity.
- Help the group navigate conflicts by working through them rather than around them.
- Support relationships in a way that allows team members to trust, value, and respect one another.
- Celebrate resolutions of conflict and successful team solutions!

Step 5.3: Discuss and Learn from Mistakes

Even the most promising solution will sometimes go badly, and the most highly committed team members will make mistakes. Mistakes represent a critical opportunity for team learning, but are often either glossed over or punished by team leaders. When mistakes are punished, team members learn to be fearful of taking risks or acting authentically from their personal wisdom. When mistakes are ignored, the same mistakes will continue to happen again and again.

Learning Organizations

As the leader of a learning organization, you must be willing to model and lead open, non-blaming communication about team failures and mistakes in a way that builds trust and enthusiasm for learning. The "Lessons Log" activity suggested in the introduction of this book can provide a useful framework for breaking down failures as a team and turning them into opportunities for learning and improved performance. Without pointing fingers, have the team discuss what should *continue,* what should *stop,* and what should *start.*

The best way to learn from mistakes is to pair a situation where things went poorly with a similar situation where things went well. Looking at both situations at the same time allows you to mine both experiences for insights and to dig deeply for the improvements that can be made. This approach will assist you in learning, as the differences between success and failure will be easier to spot by contrast than in isolation.

Wrap-up and Summary

We've presented five key leadership strategies to help you create a climate of change within your organization. In this way, you can soon be the leader of an organization that never stops learning, but is continually committed to growth. You can unlock the potential of your organization to improve and grow by using the five keys presented here.

As a review, here are those five keys to leading a powerful learning organization:

Key 1: Expand your Horizons

Key 2: Invest in People

Key 3: Retire Outdated Paradigms

Key 4: Cultivate a Shared Vision

Key 5: Tap In to the Collective

If you've found the information in this report intriguing, be sure to look carefully at the next pages to find out more about CAN-DO and what some of CAN-DO's other information products are. Each book, report and video address one or more ways you can bring new ideas to your organization, improve skills, build knowledge and solve problems. You owe it to yourself to sign up on the email list to receive notifications on the latest products that will help you lead a better organization. Go to www.uta.edu/can-do to sign up now. When you do this, you'll gain access to an exclusive report, available for free ONLY to CAN-DO subscribers.

Can We Do Something More for You?

CAN-DO! To learn more about how to develop attention-getting short reports, videos, training, and other technical assistance, contact Dr. Rick Hoefer at rhoefer@uta.edu . Dr. Hoefer is the Roy E. Dulak Professor for Community Practice Research at the School of Social Work at the University of Texas at Arlington. He directs the Center for Advocacy, Nonprofit and Donor Organizations (CAN-DO).

Dr. Hoefer specializes in translating cutting edge, best practice research into usable practice points for organizations. His passion is helping nonprofits succeed in providing high quality services to our communities. He has over 25 years of experience working in and with nonprofit organizations, assisting them in improving their services through program evaluation, advocacy, and management consulting. Dr. Hoefer has authored more than 30 published journal articles and 6 books and has given scores of presentations in the fields of nonprofit management, advocacy, program evaluation and policy practice.

Shannon Graves is a consultant with experience in nonprofit management, fund development, strategic planning, and community organizing. She specializes in bringing best practices to service systems and organizations through the effective and innovative development of policies, programs, and people.

Learn More with Video Resources by CAN-DO

For timely CAN-DO tips and resources, subscribe to Dr. Hoefer's YouTube channel by searching for DrRickHoefer. You may also visit www.uta.edu/can-do for links to these highly ranked videos:

3 Ways to Raise More Funds Online:
https://www.youtube.com/watch?v=uwOBHV8JwLc

Decision-making Flow Chart:
https://www.youtube.com/watch?v=8ptq1SR0wok

Five Steps on How to Hire an Evaluator:
https://www.youtube.com/watch?v=hMEEBZJT4uE

How to Decrease Staff Turnover:
https://www.youtube.com/watch?v=GQqhsNsfWmc

How to Handle Nonprofit Mission Drift:
https://www.youtube.com/watch?v=m5Kwa8UnRIY

How to Use Grants.gov to Find Federal Grants:
https://www.youtube.com/watch?v=yDbGerr5Oek

Leadership and Learning Organizations:
https://www.youtube.com/watch?v=fdojiqAb9Ss

The Ethics of Advocacy:
https://www.youtube.com/watch?v=4x5PnVrt5zw

What Can CAN-DO Do for You?
https://www.youtube.com/watch?v=c8YR8ivyBPo

But Wait, There's More!

Do you like this book? Be sure to check out CAN-DO's highly acclaimed previous release, *Your Organization's Riveting Story: How to Write So People Will Read, Remember, and Respond,* by Richard Hoefer and Shannon Graves. It is available on www.amazon.com as a softback book or a Kindle e-book. Save more when you buy the paperback and e-book as a bundle! Here's what reviewers have said:

"This is a great resource for anyone responsible for promoting their organization. This publication gives the reader practical tips and helps to develop a compelling story for their organization. Practical. Straightforward. Excellent!"   -Larry Watson

"From creating a vision to packaging and sharing stories, the seven step approach is easy to follow and a great resource for organizations to communicate their work more effectively."   -Christine Tucker

Starting on the next page, we've provided you an excerpt from *Your Organization's Riveting Story: How to Write So People Will Read, Remember and Respond.* To read the entire book, go to Amazon.com and search for it by name. It's a very small investment to create large scale improvements in how your organization communicates with outsiders—people who may invest heavily in YOUR organization if you follow the tips included in this book.

Excerpt From

Your Organization's Riveting Story:
How to Write So People will Read, Remember and Respond
By Richard Hoefer and Shannon Graves

●●●

Introduction: About this Report

How a Good Story Turns Readers into Donors

The goal of this report is to help you write an original, expressive, and downright riveting story about your organization. But why? The truth is that stories sell! Advertisers spend billions of dollars on their "brand" - essentially, a story about how their product makes you feel. Lexus inspires luxury and elegance. Apple recalls youth and tech savvy living. Dove Chocolates make us feel like we deserve some decadence.

Consumers and donors have something in common. We all want to invest in things that make us feel good! If you aren't telling a story that elicits powerful feelings about what your organization can do in your community, donors will open their purse strings to someone else who is. There are millions of stories out there, but we'll teach you how to make yours stand out above the rest!

How to Get the Most from This Report

We'd like to suggest a couple of ways to get the most out of this report. While there is no "wrong way" to use it, we've found that it is important to actually work through the steps as you read. If you're working on it by yourself, set aside a short amount of time each day for a week to think carefully about and complete your current step and revise your previous day's work.

At some point, you'll want to show your ideas to others and get their input, but also remember that it is usually easier for others to work from a completed draft than from partially developed ideas. Develop something that you like and can explain, and then make yourself open to feedback.

Another way to use this report is to work on it as a team. Recruit several people from your organization to complete Steps 1 and 2, and then hand off the fine tuning to one person or a designated planning team. Establish a process for approval of the final product.

However you use this report, we hope that it will inspire you to think about your organization's work in a new way! We also hope that if you have any questions about the content here or if find yourself facing challenges that are bigger than the scope of this report, that you will reach out to CAN-DO to have all your questions answered and learn how training and technical assistance from CAN-DO (www.uta.edu/can-do) may be able to help YOU.

Now, let's go through the 7 steps to creating a riveting report that people will read, remember and respond to.

Step 1: Create a Vision

The first step to telling a captivating story is creating a vision that you can actually see and describe in vibrant detail to your audience. Close your eyes. Picture your community as it would be *without* the services of your organization. What do you see? Draw it in the first box below. Don't worry - you don't have to be an artist to be successful! Use cartoons, stick figures, or printed out images from the internet to get your point across.

Here's what your community looks like without you:

If your vision isn't something you can draw or take a photo of, then look more closely. Is it an individual with a mental illness? A father spending a great deal of time away from his family in order to earn a living? A mother unable to read bedtime stories to her son? If you have a vision that you can't draw, describe on the lines below this paragraph. Use words that evoke emotions in you and your potential audience.

Learning Organizations

_____
_____
_____
_____
_____
_____
_____

Now, close your eyes again and create a new vision: A vision of a community in which *your organization has totally fulfilled its mission.* What does this community look like? Make a graphic of what your community looks like when your mission is fulfilled:

[   ]

In the lines below, describe it in detail, with passion! Go ahead... get poetic, romantic. Dream big! Your vision isn't finished yet. Ask others in your organization to complete the same activity and show you what they see. As you mold your vision, remember to keep your target audience in mind. Who are your most likely donors? What "before" and "after" visions are likely to resonate most with their fears and hopes for the community?

_____

_____

_____

_____

_____

_____

_____

_____

_____

_____

_____

_____

_____

_____

_____

Learning Organizations

A Sample Vision: Community Action for South Texas
From time to time during this report, we'll give you an example from an organization which is not real but demonstrates some common possible solutions to the questions posed here.

Vision of Community without CAST: South Texas' children are hungry, its elderly are isolated, and its workers are idle. An entire way of living is dying as rural communities suffer from infrastructure decay, economic decline, and population out-migration.

Vision Fulfilled with CAST: Rural communities throughout South Texas have the same opportunities as communities throughout the state: Infrastructure needs (including high speed internet and safe roads, highways, and bridges) are met, safe and nutritious food is consumed in proper amounts by all, young and old find common purpose in lifelong learning opportunities and legal methods to earn a living are plentiful.

[This Excerpt Skips to the End of the Book]

Wrap-up and Summary

We've presented a 7-step process to help you organize YOUR organization's story, and make it one that your stakeholders will read, remember and *RESPOND* to, with greater involvement and donations.

As a review, here are those seven steps to writing reports that people will read, remember, and respond to.

Step 1: Create a vision.

Step 2: Compile evidence.

Step 3: Work the numbers.

Step 4: Take it to the streets.

Step 5: Get visual.

Step 6: Call to action.

Step 7: Package your story, then share it.

Organizations such as yours need to be engaging and this report provides you with empirically supported ways to garner additional interest in your work, by helping YOU focus on ways to be "riveting"—yielding more connections between your organization and the people you want to connect with.

•••

Buy Your Organziation's Riveting Story: How to Write So People Read, Remember and Respond *from www.amazon.com in paperback or Kindle e-book. Buy both together as a bundle for special pricing!*

www.ingramcontent.com/pod-product-compliance
Lightning Source LLC
Chambersburg PA
CBHW071549170526
45166CB00004B/1607